All About Sports
with Inspector McQ

Written by Patty Rutland Mullins
Illustrated by Len Ebert

World Book, Inc.
a Scott Fetzer company
Chicago

All About Sports

World Book, Inc.
233 N. Michigan Avenue
Chicago, IL 60601

WORLD BOOK and the TREASURE TREE DEVICE are registered trademarks or trademarks of World Book, Inc.

ISBN 0-7166-1645-9 ISBN 0-7166-1647-5 (set)
Library of Congress Control Number: 2003116755

Printed in Malaysia
2 3 4 5 6 7 8 9 08 07 06

For information about other World Book publications, visit our Web site **http://www.worldbook.com** or call **1-800-WORLDBK (967-5325).** For information about sales to schools and libraries, call **1-800-975-3250 (United States); 1-800-837-5365 (Canada).**

Cover design by Rosa Cabrera
Book design by George Wenzel
Inspector McQ illustrated by Eileen Mueller Neill
Photo, page 6, © Louis Capozzola, Focus on Sports
Photo, page 8, Henry & Janet Grosshandler
Photos, page 10, The Topps Company, Inc.—Chicago White Sox trademark reproduced with permission of Major League Baseball Properties
Photo, page 11, Cincinnati Reds
Photo, page 13, Index Stock
Photo, page 14, © Cornell University
Photo, page 17, Focus on Sports
Photo, page 25, Focus on Sports
Photo, page 30, © David Madison, Duomo
World Book photo, page 31, by Steve Spicer

Are you ready to work with me?
In this book, we will look into some very
interesting sports cases.
Have you ever wondered why you might
play tee ball before baseball, how football
started, why swimmers don't sink, why bike
wheels are so skinny, and . . . well,
probably lots of other things?
Come on, grab your tennis shoes and let's
get going!

What is the world's most popular sport ?

Take a guess. If you guessed soccer, you would be right.

Nations have a national anthem and a national flag. They also have a national sport. Soccer takes that honor in most European and Latin American countries. In fact, people play soccer on almost every continent in the world—in North America and South America, Europe, Asia, Africa, and Australia. Soccer is truly an international sport.

In the United States, this game is called soccer, and football is a game with an oval-shaped ball. In many other countries, however, soccer is called football, and the U.S. game is called American football.

The history of soccer holds a rich store of legend and lore from around the world. No one knows exactly where the sport began. However, citizens in ancient China and Greece played an early form of the game.

And picture this: In the Middle Ages, the time of kings and queens, and knights in shining armor, entire towns would battle each other in a game of soccer on fields as big as a town! The game was dangerous and wild, so some kings tried to ban it.

4

What is a fast-growing team sport for kids

You can be an inspector and help me on this one.
Here are the clues:

6

1. This sport is played in more countries than any other in the world.

2. Many players learn the game as children.

3. Even young children can learn the plays and moves of this sport. Its rules are among the easiest to master of any team sport.

4. You do not have to be especially tall or extra strong to play.

5. Both girls and boys play.

6. The sport involves kicking a ball downfield. Kicking a ball comes naturally to children.

7. Most any round, bouncy ball will do. You do not need official gear to practice this sport. Nor do you need an official field to play.

So, what sport are we talking about? Of course, it's soccer! The world's most popular sport is one of the fastest growing team sports for kids today in the United States.

How did tee ball start❓

A white flash speeds toward you. Crack! You hit a home run! Making a dream like this one come true begins with tee ball, a game for young players, ages 5–8. It is the official warm-up game for baseball played by older children. Let's go see a game.

Step up to home plate. It has an adjustable pole in the center. You place a baseball on top of the pole. The coach shows you how to hold and swing the bat. Sometimes you swing in slow motion, stopping just short of the ball. You are training your eyes and hands to work together. In a game, you take a good, practiced swing and, hopefully, smack the ball. Then you run the bases. Go!

Now I don't remember tee ball from my younger days. How did it all get started? Aha . . . my sources report that tee ball has become more popular for kids in the last 30 years or so. Moms, dads, and coaches wanted beginning baseball to be safer—without wild pitches hitting kids just as they were learning to play.

Meanwhile, professional baseball player and Hall of Famer Branch Rickey developed the tee-ball system in the 1950's, when he was a recruiter for the Dodgers. He wanted to help players practice batting. The idea caught on and, in the 1970's, the Little League made tee ball part of its beginning baseball program. It's been a "hit" ever since!

9

How did baseball get its start ?

L et's investigate. I'm off to the Baseball Hall of Facts to find out about baseball's beginning.

Fact #1: People still argue about where baseball started. Some people say baseball was invented by Abner Doubleday in Cooperstown, New York. But my sources are quite certain that baseball really came from an old English game called rounders.

Fact #2: Alexander Cartwright made up the first official rules for baseball in 1845.

Fact #3: Baseball teams began to form. Team names like the Cincinnati Red Stockings and the Chicago White Stockings remind us of names we use today: the Reds and the White Sox.

Fact #4: One early official rule was: Do NOT throw the ball at a player to put him out. Ouch, I say!

Fact #5: Today, pitchers try to outsmart batters. In early baseball, a batter "ordered" a pitch; the pitcher delivered it. Times have changed!

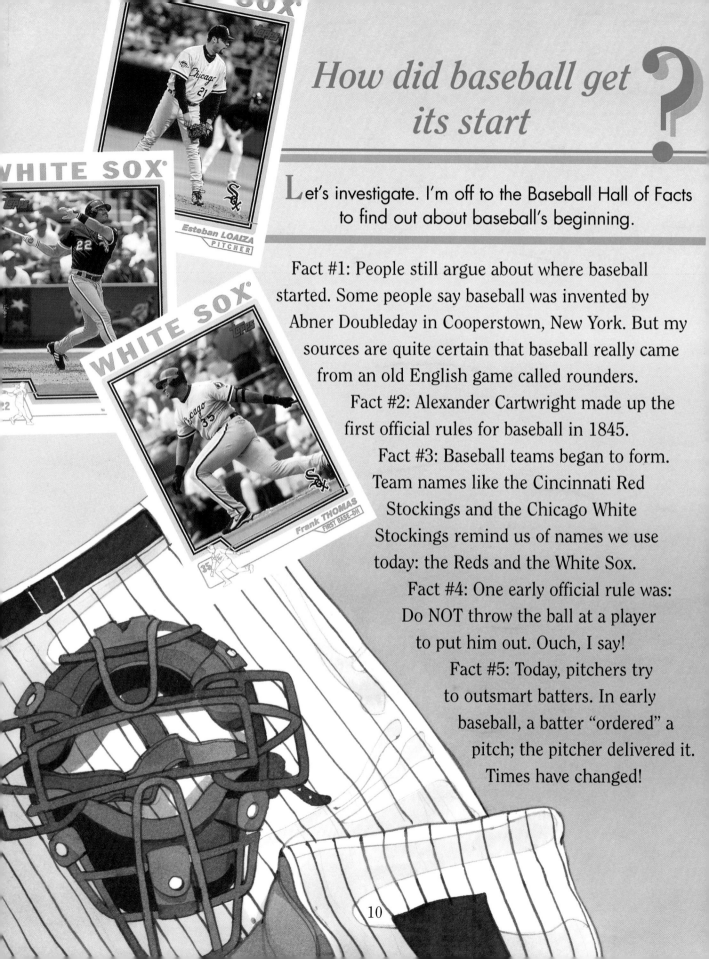

Esteban LOAIZA
PITCHER

Frank THOMAS
FIRST BASE–DH

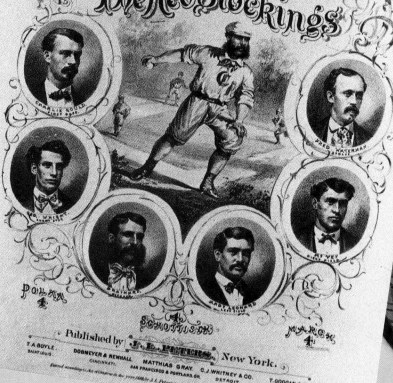

Why are baseball and football seasons different?

My first answer would be: "Because it has always been that way." And I would be right. Playing baseball in summer and football in fall is a strong tradition in the United States.

But as an inspector, I want to know *how* the tradition came to be. I suspect the weather played a big part. Rainy or snowy weather would make seeing a white baseball in the air very difficult.

That would make it hard to hit the ball. As you know, batting the ball is the main way to score runs in baseball.

An American football is much bigger than a baseball. Players can see it better in bad weather. Also, players do not bat it through the air. They can carry it or hand it to someone to move it nearer to the goal.

This tradition may never change because it is so handy. Baseball season ends about the time football season begins. Football season winds down about the time basketball season begins. And, basketball season winds down about the time baseball season begins! Fans of these sports like this.

How did football start ?

Master Miles McQ, my great-great-grandfather, loved football. Peering and cheering through blades of grass, he watched the first football games more than a hundred years ago.

With no bleachers, people sat in buggies or stood around the field. The field stretched three times longer than today. Teams had 25 players, compared to 11 now. "Football" was really another name for soccer. The ball was round. Players could not carry or throw it down-field. But Gramps McQ spoke of a college game that changed football forever.

In 1874, Harvard University played McGill University, from Canada. The teams played soccer-

style football and rugby-style football. In English rugby, players catch and run with an almond-shaped ball. Harvard liked the rugby-style game better and it began to catch on.

Later, a player from Yale University, Walter Camp, helped make football what it is today. He thought of having a quarterback handle the ball each play. And he invented the system of "downs." In 1906, players first used the forward pass, which made football more exciting to watch.

I wish I'd been with Gramps in the early days of football!

15

Why is a touchdown called a touchdown ?

Ready for the best moment in football? I'm here at a game. LOOK! A player has caught the ball and carried it across the goal line. Touchdown! His team scores six points.

Touchdowns are such glorious moments! And the word "touchdown" sounds so right. Here's what I found out about it:

The word "touchdown" comes from an early after-touchdown custom. Whoever carried the ball across the goal line bent down, touched the ball to the ground, then handed it to the referee. This was a signal to the fans that a touchdown had happened.

How did basketball get its start ?

The invention of basketball in 1891 was a nice piece of work by YMCA instructor James Naismith. As I found out the facts, I imagined myself watching an early game . . .

McQ: Inspector McQ here, coming to you from the YMCA Training School in Springfield, Massachusetts. Good show down there, players, but what are you doing?

Players: Throwing soccer balls into peach baskets, of course (old-fashioned, brown soccer balls).

McQ: Baskets! Aha . . . so we have "basket ball."

Players: That's right. Our teacher, James Naismith, invented this exciting game to be played indoors.

McQ: I note that the clever Naismith took clues from popular outdoor games: driving a ball into a goal; having a center line dividing each team's turf. However, a gym floor is a lot harder than grass. So there is no rough contact or tackling in basketball.

Players: These balls don't bounce well!

McQ: If basketball catches on, a new ball *is* in order. I'll try to think of something.

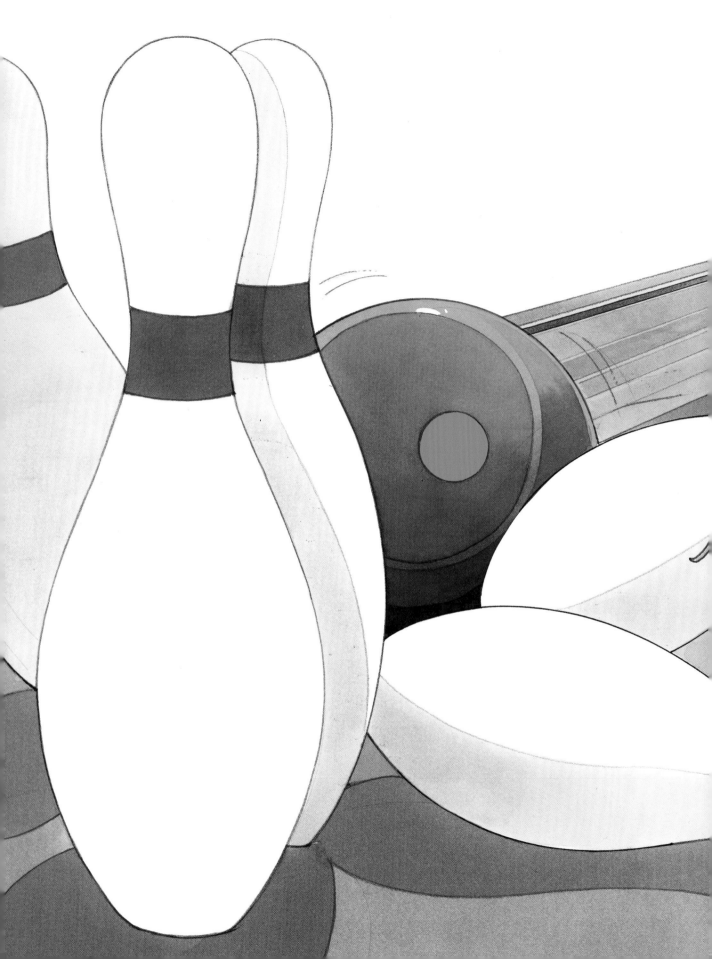

Did you know bowling is an ancient sport?

Kids and grown-ups have been having bowling fun for centuries. Here's what I found out about this popular sport.

Scientists once found a bowling ball and pins in Egypt in the tomb of a little girl that had lived some 7,000 years ago. She had used a round stone for a ball and nine long stones for pins. Early bowlers stacked three blocks of marble to make an archway. Then they rolled the ball through the opening toward the pins.

Today, the basic shape of the pins is the same: long and tall. Our plastic-coated wooden pins have flat bottoms, heavier than the tops, so they do not tip over by accident. Only a rolling ball or other tipping pins can knock the pins down. A bar sweeps downed pins off the lane and, at the end of a turn, a machine replaces them with ten more pins. Before there were automatic machines, pinsetters grabbed the pins after each bowler's turn and set them up again.

21

How do swimmers stay afloat?

Let's watch a home movie of my first swimming lesson in the neighborhood pool. Would I sink or swim? I was a bit afraid, I must say. But my friend Amy explained how we float and made swimming seem easy.

See me splashing? Water feels loose and slippery. Actually, it is strong enough to hold some things up, like my sailboat. This is "buoyancy." Buoyancy is "floating power."

At the same time, our weight is pressed down on the water by a force called "gravity." Buoyancy pushes us up and gravity pushes us down. Luckily, buoyancy wins. Most people float naturally.

Look, Amy shows me how to move my arms
and kick my legs. There I go! The faster and
stronger I become, the farther I can swim. Not
bad for a beginning mouse swimmer! Let's go
take a look at some divers next.

How do divers keep their balance?

Here I am at a diving meet. What a spectacular event! Divers don't just jump into the water. They may twist, turn, spin, flip, and speed through the air—and with such grace. How do they do it?

This is what I've observed: The key to a perfect dive is in the balance. Divers lose points if they cannot keep their balance on the board. Tripping or tilting brings a penalty. So, to be safe and to score high, divers follow exact rules for each step in a dive: the start, take-off, flight, and entry into the water. Balance is especially important in the first two steps.

See how divers keep their heads and bodies straight as they begin a take-off? This helps them keep their balance. Depending upon the kind of dive, they may hold their arms out, down, in front, or up high. Correct arm position helps to steady the divers for their flight. Flight? With good balance and years of practice, divers can seem to fly without wings. Bravo!

24

What are the Olympics ?

"Swifter, higher, stronger." That is the motto of the Olympic Games, a world sports event that happens one winter and one summer every four years.

The finest young athletes from all over the world train for years to be part of this spectacular event. Then they hope for their moment of glory—maybe a gold medal for the 100-meter run, for swimming, diving, figure skating, or any other of several sports.

The name "Olympics" comes from the birthplace of the event. These games began on the plains of Olympia in ancient Greece almost 2,800 years ago.

In ancient Greece, the contestants promised to play fairly and to be "good sports," just like now.

The Olympic Games teach everyone, not just athletes, two important lessons: First, in whatever you do, try to do your best. And second, people of the world can get together, even compete against each other, in the spirit of peace and friendship.

Good show, all the way around!

Why are the wheels on racing bicycles so thin ?

Today's the big day. I'm in France watching the world-famous bike race, the Tour de France. That's biking's "tour de force," French for "act of strength."

Racers ride for around three weeks, covering about 2,500 miles (4,000 km) total. The destination: Paris!

They need a special bike for this race, where speed is king. One year, a racer won by just 8 seconds!

Notice how skinny a racing bike's wheels look. The invention of thin wheels has made it possible for racing bikes to go faster. Bikes must fight a natural force that's everywhere: friction. When two things rub against each other, friction happens. Friction slows motion. The more tire that touches the road, the more friction results. Thick wheels create more friction than thin wheels. So, thick-wheeled bikes go slower.

They're off! Any chance of my catching up?

What is gymnastics ?

Gymnastics. Hmmm. That makes me think of running, jumping, flipping. I'm getting dizzy just thinking of it. Obviously, gymnastics is not a sport for mice. But it is a wonderful sport for some graceful, hard-working friends of mine. Come along. Let's visit a gym and see them work out.

Watch as my friend Kim demonstrates. See her on the balance beam? Kim points her fingers and toes just so and does all sorts of "balancing acts." Gymnasts are so graceful that they can run, leap, and turn around on this narrow beam. Then they might try other equipment—such as the uneven parallel bars— swinging and swooping like trapeze artists. Over a padded "horse" known as the side horse, I've seen Kim take a running, jumping start and soar through the air.

My other friend Eric is here, too. Hanging onto two rings, he will swing and flip his body, performing wonders. Maybe he'll do a pommel horse event next. The pommel horse is like Kim's side horse, only it has handles on top. Eric would hold onto the handles and swing his legs around and around the horse. Bravo, my friends! Your strength and grace are beautiful!

30

Whew! What a workout!
I couldn't be out of breath, could I? Well,
maybe a little. But all that work was worth it.
Think of the many new sports facts we know!
I'm sure I'll get my second wind in time to
investigate the next set of cases.
Join me, won't you?